Let's Talk About
BEING FORGETFUL

Distributed by:

Word, Incorporated
4800 W. Waco Drive
Waco, TX 76703

Copyright © 1984 by Joy Berry

Printed in the United States of America
ISBN 0881490210

Let's Talk About
BEING FORGETFUL

By JOY BERRY

Illustrated by John Costanza

Edited by Kate Dickey

Designed by Abigail Johnston

Living Skills Press
Fallbrook, California

Let's talk about BEING FORGETFUL.

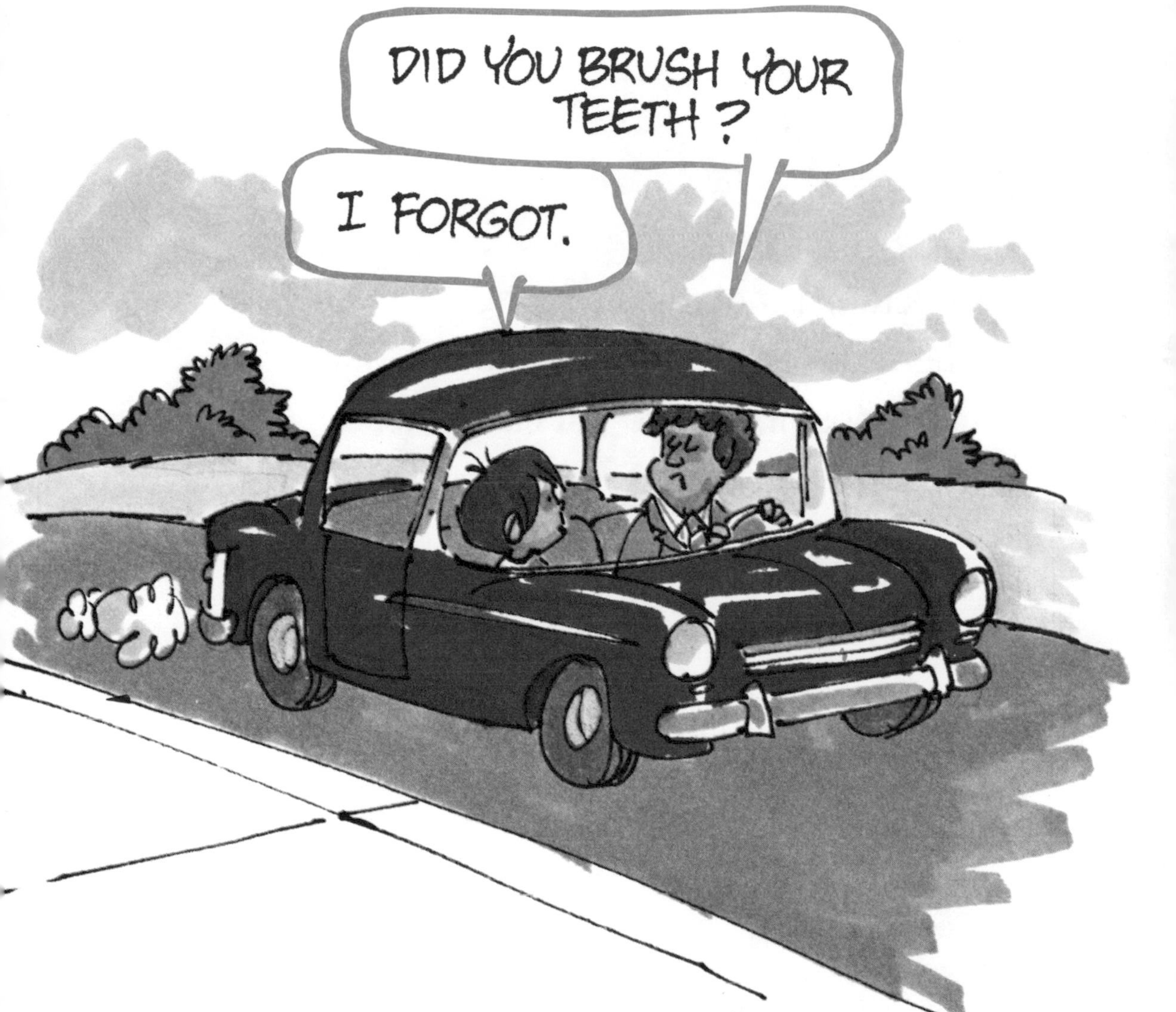
DID YOU BRUSH YOUR TEETH?
I FORGOT.

Forgetting is not remembering.
When you forget something you do not
think about it. You do not remember it.

Have you ever forgotten to do something?

Have you ever forgotten to tell someone something?

Have you ever forgotten to take something with you?

Have you ever forgotten and left something behind?

Forgetting something can frustrate you.

It can frustrate others as well.

You can avoid being forgetful.

There are things you can do to help you remember.

Get in the habit of asking yourself this question before you go from place to place:

"Am I forgetting anything?"

Ask someone to remind you about something you do not want to forget.

Write yourself a note to help you remember something.

Pin it to yourself, or put it in a place where you are sure to see it.

Write yourself a note or make a reminder
mark on the back of your hand so that
you won't forget something. You can
use a washable ink pen to do this.

Tie a string around your finger. Make sure you do not tie it too tightly. The string will feel uncomfortable. As you become aware of it, you will remember to do what you need to do. If you do not want to use string, you can use a bandaid.

Put things in a special place so that you will not forget to take them with you. A good place is next to the door through which you'll be leaving.

Being forgetful can be frustrating.

It is important that you try not to forget things.